MW01195112

INTRODUCTION

Dear reader, by ordering this book you are saying to me that you have a dream, a vision, and a mandate to fulfill. You are demonstrating that this mandate you have, you believe to be God inspired! You would not desire to become a religious non-profit organization unless you believed that. Any vision and dream is worth the price and sacrifice to obtain the prize. I wish you all the wisdom and knowledge you need to fulfill what you have been entrusted to do.

This book is being written because of a need. It is a need I personally had when I began in the Pastoral Ministry in 1986. The Bible School I attended did not prepare us in many of the practical areas of ministry at the time though I am told they are doing better in that area today. It was not only my Bible College but many others as well have taught only the Bible and not the financials or legal aspects of the ministry that are just as imperative for success. Many others still that are in ministry today did not have any formal training.

It won't take long out there in the ministry field to figure out that the messenger needs tools to build along with training in the Holy Scriptures. It has been a great personal burden in my life to achieve the goals I have had without a proper road map. However, by having that experience, it has birthed another burden to lift others and give them some guidelines that can set them on the right track, especially those in Independent works. This book will offer you some input from the "other side". I do not claim to be an expert but, I have learned a few things along the way that I hope will be of benefit to you the reader.

1

I hope that you hear my heart throughout and know that what I am sharing is not an iron clad do's and don'ts. But rather it is a guideline to help you as a Visionary or Pioneer to head in the right directions and ask the right questions. What I have learned has come from personal experience and gleaning from the successes and failures of others. Gaining such knowledge will give you a step ahead that will help you gain more ground at a faster rate than those who have come before you.

So take a look and I pray that this book offers you many rich insights and a hand up to what you desire to accomplish so that you may fulfill your God given Destiny. In order to fulfill our destiny we need faith, patience and foreknowledge coupled with obedience. God can use those who will make themselves available and follow His leading. May the Lord give you grace to achieve all that is set before you to further His kingdom and His plan in the earth. My pray is that this book will help you to achieve that goal.

CHAPTER ONE

WHAT EVERY NON-PROFIT LEADER
NEEDS TO KNOW

Welcome to the Ministry! I hope you bought this book at just the right time. One of the greatest faults in ministerial training is the lack of teaching on how a church should be run governmentally. Most Ministers are not often prepared for the legal aspect they will face in Ministry. To every ministry there is a spiritual and a natural side. Both are very important when it comes to being responsible for the lives of others of whom you will give account.

This training is lacking the most in Independent, Charismatic and Full Gospel circles and private para church organizations. The other denominational churches simply have a governing structure in place that you "step into" whether you wish to or not. But for the Independent or Apostolic Ministry, as you pioneer your ministry, you have to have a starting place in your governing structure that you can both begin with and grow into.

In this book, I hope to share with you some concepts and thoughts about these things that you may not have faced yet. In the future, as this world waxes cold and dark as we see the coming of our Lord approaching, you will need to be equipped to handle many complex situations.

I hope to answer some questions for you such as; By Laws, Constitutions, Policies, etc so that you can build or restructure your ministry into a healthy organism that brings glory and honor to God.

Structure; what its purpose is and why do we need it? Everything we do should be done in excellence and integrity. Most desire to walk uprightly but don't know how to set their organization up in a way that promotes that kind of thing to happen. When I began in the ministry over 30 years ago, my first thought was that I didn't need any documents and By-Laws certainly weren't necessary. After all aren't we ALL Christians here? Won't we all just do the "right" thing? Well, much to my surprise, "the right thing" comes in many different shapes and forms even in the non-profit sector. I just believed that everyone was honest and desired integrity to be their highest ambition. Boy! Was I sadly mistaken? You see not every church member or board members come from God. Yes, that's right; in fact some of them seem to be the devil himself clothed in flesh.

God has many things to say in the His Word concerning ethics and integrity, honesty and virtue. If everyone followed these precepts and guidelines laid out in the Word of God, let's face it we would have won the world by now. Instead, every day another Minister falls, every day, the name of Christ is defamed by the behavior of a Christian leader or his followers.

When I left Bible School, I was sure I would win the world or at least my first city in a day, ok, maybe a year. But never in my wildest dreams did I ever expect believers in the house of God to act unbecomingly or in any kind of misconduct.

This book has been written to help you not to go through some of the painful things many other Ministers of grace with a heart as big as the world like yours have suffered. It is my heart to give you valuable information that will protect your Ministry from the wolves and the vulchers that Satan sends. To ward off the evil influences that come to kill steal and destroy what God is doing in and through your life as a Minister to the people whom God has sent you to reach, love and disciple.

My friend if you are reading this booklet it is most likely because you are not sure how to set up a nonprofit ministry or because you have been brutally mistreated as a servant of God because the governments you had on paper did not facilitate the dream you held within your heart. You may be someone who has taken over a pre-existing ministry with improper structure or you have left a denomination that has held you back from obtaining your God given vision. Perhaps you see things that are not just right but you are not certain how to correct them and you have created your own monster that you need to slay.

My greatest hope is that many of you are just getting started and you will find treasures of information within these pages to help you make good solid decisions for years to come never having to rebuild or reconstruct which causes a loss of time which is most precious in these last days.

Someone once said to me, "it is far easier to build a house brand new rather than to renovate it." The things written on these pages are to help churches who desire order and understanding about tax exempt purposes and privileges. This does not apply to any other organization such as an evangelistic organization. These types of organizations are under a separate set of guidelines by the government due to their structural nature and I am not knowledgeable about such things. This information applies solely to church structure and organizations.

I suggest that if you are looking at a traveling type ministry that you have a church 501 C (3) recognized to be your home base and run your ministry under their tax exempt umbrella to avoid scandalous accusations and lack of accountability that other such ministry have fallen prey to over the past years. Due to the abuse of such organizations in the past I am told the IRS is not very favorable of such ministries being independent and that it is very hard to obtain nowadays. It is advisable to set up such a ministry as an extension of a local church organization or charter type ministry under already established organizations.

When it comes to church government most people are in the dark so to speak as to how they should set up their Ministry. In this book, I will share with you some sample By Laws and ask you to consider the things necessary to fulfill God's very best for you and for those you will lead.

There is nothing more frustrating to people who want to get involved, not to know the boundaries that will guide them and the structure that will bring order. For any ministry to be healthy it must have one leader and many followers. Yet within those followers many under shepherds or those with delegated power must be appointed to ever bring stability and growth that we all desire to obtain. After all, we are building the Kingdom of God and we are striving to bring as many souls in as possible before the Lord returns.

No true shepherd desires to win thirty souls and no more. Of course not, a true shepherd will desire to keep growing, keep reaching until all are reached within his or her power. Without order and guidelines we will find that a vision of something greater than ourselves cannot be obtained.

I do not claim to be one who has figured it all out. I only wish to share my thoughts and discoveries with anyone desirous of the information that will help them to reach higher and farther should the Lord tarry. I am not a legal consultant nor do I have full knowledge of laws within each state. However, the information I share in these pages with you has been developed out of many painstaking hours of revisions and restructuring that have been approved over and over by the IRS for churches. They are also written with the visionary in mind as well as the flock. I would advise you to take your finished product by the eyes of seasoned Ministers and Attorneys of law that may find something that needs tweaking.

I am at best a Minister/Missionary who has traveled a long road of improper By Laws and structure in Ministry that has caused me to work diligently at finding something that is strong and effective. I am a person who has had no choice but to learn at the hands of experience; experiences that attributed to frustration, disillusionment, and finally, wisdom. Because of my struggle it has become a personal burden of my heart to help others who are unknowledgeable as I once was, so that they can move ahead quickly and effectively in their calling unhindered and free to be all God desires them to be.

Most people think that a minister should know everything, unwilling to realize that we too are simply human beings with frailties and weaknesses. It is my prayer that this book will give you understanding and give you a wealth of information that I have had to find by digging during my 30 years in ministerial work. May the Lord bless this endeavor and bring truth that sets men free!

CHAPTER TWO

THE FIRST STEP

Every organization needs a few things to get started with a proper structure.

The first thing one must do to begin building is to form a Corporation. What is a Corporation? A Corporation limits liability to the Corporation only in any kind of legal matter and not against personal assets. Establishing a Corporation also gives the legal right for that Ministry or Corporation to enter into contracts especially where buying and selling property is concerned. This is when your Articles of Incorporation are created. This is the easiest of all applications.

Becoming a Corporation sounds like a difficult task but actually it is very simple. You would apply through each state as an Ecclesiastical Corporation. For example, in most states you will find a bureau of commercial services. There are a few questions to answer such as location and purpose which are contained in your Articles of Incorporation. This does not make you tax exempt it simply makes you an identifiable entity. Your corporation should consist of a minimum of three unrelated people to make up your Board of Directors. At least half of your board should not be related. The purpose for this is to protect the keeping of a majority in the eyes of the IRS. However, don't appoint people just because they are friends or who you think will be a "YES" man. But, definitely appoint someone who has your best interest as their foremost objective and someone who owns your vision not their own. Make sure this person or persons have a good track record in character and integrity.

As for the next step which is drawing up Articles of Incorporation, this too is not a difficult step and today I am going to make it very easy for you in the words that the IRS will take a liking to. There are some very basic things that the IRS is looking for in the language of your Articles. The IRS wants to be sure that your organization is an interment one. That is to say that you will gain no private benefit but your organization is for the benefit of others with no political activity involved.

Although you may be involved in political things as a church, you are not allowed to have a substantial lobbying above 5% of your overall annual income. My question to you here is; though we want to stand for what is right, it is not necessary to provide income through a tax exempt organization to do so? The government calls this the separation of church and state. I believe it is a good policy and should be honored.

You must ask yourself what is the reason our organization was formed? Was it for the betterment of people or for politics? I do not disregard the importance of believers being actively involved in government and moral issues however it should be done without the funds of the local church which is for the purpose of evangelism not the financial backing of a said candidate running for office or for the passing of laws. These things should be maintained through other venues and activist organizations and should be privately supported by believers in the body of Christ is my opinion on this matter and very well looked upon by the IRS I might add.

Another thing mentioned in your Articles, is to give your Organization the power to buy and obtain properties for your Ministry. They will state that you have the power to enter into contracts and make money to run your said Ministry following the guidelines of the law. These Articles also state that only reasonable compensation will be rendered and that funds obtained will not be used for personal gain. They will also state that you will not discriminate based on sex, age, race or handicap.

One of the last clauses will be that if you were to dissolve your Organization that your assets will be distributed to other 501 C(3) organizations like yourself and not distributed to individuals for personal gain. These things are very important to the IRS as they are safe guarding the community from being mislead in their charitable gifts as well as disallowing illegal tax shelters to individuals under the guise of a Tax-Exempt Organization.

Along with filing your Articles of Incorporation to the IRS in a language that is required by them with the clauses afore mentioned, your next step is to file an application to receive an EIN number. This is a number given you by the IRS and becomes your identification number to them. It is like a social security number to identify your Organization and is necessary to be able to open a bank account in the name of your Corporation. Again, you are still not recognized with the government as a Tax – Exempt Organization at this point. This EIN number which simply stands for Employer Identification

Number and is obtained by filling out a SS4 form which can be found from a website called IRS.gov home page. These two actions of applying for a Corporation and applying for an EIN number can be done simultaneously. The first application will be filed with the state in which you are located, the second, EIN, being filed with the IRS.

Listed below is a sample of Articles of Incorporation that are *pleasing* to the IRS.

Article 1

The (Board of Trustees) working in accordance with the purpose of the Organization shall comprise the (Board of Directors) as an individual and as a Director during his/her term of service to the Corporation. They must be subject to and act consistent with the purposes of the Organization. (these names in parentheses can be called by any number of names.) Such as the Advisory Board, Local Church Board, Local Presbytery etc. *(I will discuss these titles in a later chapter when we get to by laws as to their importance.)*

Article 2

AIMS

(In this article you should mention the aim of your organization in a broader sense than what you may begin with and what you may grow into so that it gives you the ability to operate in the whole of your vision. Not doing this initially will cause you to have to revise your Articles later which causes aggravation if you don't have time or the support of your collaborators, who may not completely own your vision at the time of expansion. It is better to "cover all the bases" in the beginning if possible and to be realistic, the not everyone will be spiritually minded all the time. In fact, most of the time you will deal with natural thinking people who do not have the same anointing or grace that you do, to see the whole picture as you do as a visionary.)

Example: The Ministry charges (name of church) under the direction of the residing Pastor, to preach the Gospel and provide sound Biblical teachings. We will provide community social services and community work that restores dignity to people. This ministry is designed to transform the lives of men and women and children, by re-directing their lives into positive directions based on the teachings of the Holy Scriptures. We aim to teach men practical ethics such as how to be productive husbands and fathers and women how to be productive wives and mothers of their children, to the building up and strengthening of the family unit. We aim to teach the basic principles of the Bible and offer assistance to the needy in the society that persons should apply in their lives to be strong leaders benefiting their families and their local community.

This Corporation is filing exempt under section 501 C(3) of the Internal Revenue Code, of 1954 or the corresponding provision of any future United States Internal Revenue Law. This Organization is strictly for charitable, religious and educational purposes, including for such purposes as may be deemed necessary by the Directors and as set out in the statues or provision of Section 501 C (3), pertaining to exempt organizations.

Article 3

This Corporation shall have and exercise all rights and power conferred on Non – Profit Corporations under the Law of the state of ( ) which may include without limiting the generality of the foregoing the power to: solicit, collect, receive, acquire, hold and invest money and property, both real and personal or otherwise: to sell and convert property of the Corporation and income, rents, issues and profits derived from any property of the Corporation and the proceeds for any purpose for which the Corporation was formed; to purchase, acquire, construct , own, hold, improve, and rehabilitate, or encumber real and personal property; to enter into, make, perform, and carry out contracts, partnerships and joint venture with any person, firm association or Corporation, municipality, county, state, territory, governmental, or subdivision.

Article 4

No substantial part of the activities of the Corporation shall be carrying on of propaganda, or otherwise attempting to influence legislation. The Corporation shall not participate in, or intervene in (including the publishing for distribution of statement), any political campaign on the behalf of any candidate for public office, notwithstanding any other provision of these articles. The Corporation shall not carry on any other activities not permitted to be carried out on (A) by a Corporation exempt from Federal Income Tax under Section 501 C (3) of the United States Internal Revenue Code of 1954 or (the corresponding provisions of any future United States Internal Revenue Law) employees, directors and clients shall be provided opportunities without discrimination because of race, creed, color, handicap, sex, religion or political affiliation or belief.

Article 5

This Corporation as a Non- Profit Corporation, shall be Non-stock, and no dividend, no pecuniary profits shall be declared or paid to persons thereof. The Corporation shall have and exercise all rights and power conferred, including power to contract, rent, buy or sell personal property. It does not contemplate the distribution of gains or profits to thereof and is organized solely for nonprofit purposes. The property, assets, profit and net income of this corporation are irremovably dedicated to charitable and educational purposes an no part of profits or net income of this Corporation shall ever inure to the benefits of any director, officer thereof, or other private persons, except that the Corporation shall be authorized and empowered to pay reasonable compensation for services rendered and to make payments and distributions in furtherance for the purposes of the Organization,. Upon dissolution of the Corporations, its' Directors shall after paying or making provision for payment of all debts and liabilities for the Corporation dispose of all the assets of the Corporation exclusively for the purpose of the Corporation in such a manner, or to such organizations organized and operated exclusively for charitable and educational purposes, and shall at that time qualify as an exempt organization under Section 501 C (3) of the Internal Revenue Code of 1954 law. The private property of the Directors shall not be subject to the payment of the Corporation's debt.

CHAPTER THREE

CONSTRUCTING YOUR CONSTITUTION
AND STATEMENT OF PURPOSE

Now we are going to move on to the next step in our process of structure for a non- profit organization to be strong and healthy. The first question needing to be answered is; "What is the Constitution for?" The word constitution stands for an organization, formation or structure. So in this section you are going to give a *wide* overview of the whole aim and purpose of your existence as and organization. Another name for this would be called your Mission Statement. What are you hoping to accomplish?

In your Constitution you will share what your true Mission is and in your Statement of Purpose you will give deeper definition to that mission and how it will be carried out. This Vision needs to be wider than what you even imagine you will accomplish for your freedom to grow. Remember the scriptures tell us that God is able to do exceedingly abundantly above what we could even ask or think. So dream big! Listen below you will find a sample of what your Constitution and Statement of Purpose should look like.

SAMPLE CONSTITUION AND STATEMENT OF PURPOSE

We the family that makes up the (name of church_____)
have a mission to accomplish. That mission is the reach the
world in our time for Jesus Christ through the preaching of the
Gospel. The great commission of Jesus Christ remains our
challenge, evangelism our main occupation. More clearly
defined, firstly the state of ( ), then the nation and the other
countries of the world. Most importantly to take the gospel to
those who have never heard it.

It is our prayer that this ministry grows and God raises up more
men and women to reach the entire world for His kingdom. He
will supply the men and women whose vision will not be aimed
by titles or name and positions, but will fulfill the challenge to
reach the world as one body and one team for our God through
the preaching of the un-compromised word of God in season
and out of season as God Himself apportions grace to each one.
We also pray that children yet unborn will catch the vision and
reach the lost souls here in the U.S, and beyond. That our seed
too shall be mighty in the earth should the Lord tarry His
imminent return.

The Great Commission of Christ remains our challenge,
evangelism our goal. We have a vision to carry the gospel to
everyone that is lost, we have a mission of love and compassion,
and we must reach the lost. Piercing the night with the light of
truth, pointing the way to the cross, we must reach the lost. It is
our prayer that everyone who gives his life to Christ through our
ministry will have this same vision of evangelism as his main
aim.

OBJECTIVES:

1. To preach the un-compromised message of the Gospel in all parts of the world - evangelism our main occupation.
2. To establish a local church that will reach out to our community, our county our state and the world. Our main intent will be the teaching of the Word of God and strengthening of families, morality and human dignity aiding our community in Christian service.
3. To train, ordain and license and disciple candidates for the work of the gospel ministry.
4. To establish and maintain parochial, Bible Institutes, training centers, and other religious oriented institutions such as prayer and healing schools, day care, and vocations schools as the Lord so leads us.
5. To print, publish and distribute religious materials.
6. To engage in social and community work that restores dignity to people. To establish and maintain facilities for those in need and under privileged
7. To promote a sense of understanding and mutual co-operations among the generality of Christians irrespective of their denominational affiliation, race, social status, sex, age, or handicap.
8. To allow others to affiliate/ associate and join with this ministry who have like vision and unity of purpose both nationally and abroad, joining together to fulfill the great commission of Jesus Christ.
9. To provide a structure of order that will both protect and liberate and bring guidance, alliance and accountability as well as fellowship for those enlisted in God's service.

I would encourage you as an organization to be reviewing these objectives from time to time to be sure that you are staying focused on the mission God has given to you. This review helps one from going off course and staying on a straight path. As leaders we must always ask ourselves not, "What is popular?" but rather, "What is right?"

If we stay focused upon God's mandates we will not be so easily tossed to and fro by every wind of doctrine or every passing fad or every boisterous church member pushing for "their" program. We will stay steady and on course as well as on times the things of God.

CHAPTER FOUR

BY LAWS

Now it is time to draw up your By Laws. The By Laws are one of the most important documents you will hold for your organization. These documents set forth the governing structure, making clear the code of how things are going to be carried out within your corporation and where the final authority lies. They are written down to be used as a map. By Laws are not for our everyday use. You should not have to look at a piece of paper continually to know where you are going but you still need a guideline for the purpose of a proper flow of things. By Laws are for guidance on how to proceed when conflict arises or when serious decisions must be made. Many people have said that this paperwork is for times of war not peace. By Laws are very important to the IRS when applying for tax –exemption status. They want to be sure you know how you are going to handle problems when they arise and that you have standards and principles of authority set in place. The IRS does not dictate this structure. In fact you are basically on your own as to how you set it up but there are some important aspects as a ministry you need to be aware of and safe guard yourself against unnecessary grief.

The first question you have to ask yourself is who will be the ultimate authority other than God for this organization? Believe me that is a loaded question. It is especially frustrating if you begin by asking others opinion on the matter. If you were to walk into ten assemblies of believers today, you would find 200 different answers to this question. This was a very irritating thing to me when I first came into full time ministry and began planting churches. What was the right answer? Why didn't those who instructed me in the scriptures have the same answer? Why didn't everyone agree on the same system of leadership? After much painful experience I came to find out the answer. The answer to this question is really quite simple without the opinion of people. The answer; "To whom did God give the vision?"

Depending where people have been instructed or raised up religiously, many different beliefs have been formed, not from the scriptures but rather from the pattern of the corporate world and the traditions of men. These ideals span from committees, to trustees, theocracy, to founding fathers, eldership rule, plurality of leaders, to democracies of voting and letting popularity of opinion rule to board run which could be any number of crazy ideas.

Yes, all these ideas and many more have been presented. To my knowledge most of these presented have caused more damage than good.

Many churches have begun with any one of these types of governments thinking it was a good starting point however, when trouble rose up, the WRONG person was in charge and used their power to destroy rather than build. Many have lost their ministry in one single meeting due to improper structure. They were the same people that said, "It will never happen to us." At this point in time it was too late to change the bylaws.

Others started with one form of government and found it did not facilitate the structure and order they needed but those in power *were not willing to change with the season or time* and the Minster's hands were tied to do what God had asked them to do. The man or woman of God now becomes a hireling rather than an oracle of God and has to run their God given ministry by the opinions and actions of those he or she has given the power to.

Another important fact to consider in this regard is this. The person, who holds the power of the finances, guides or controls the vision. For example, you give the treasurer or clerk of the church ultimate authority to handle the money because you as the pastor do not want to be accused of mishandling funds or stealing from God or the people.

Now, God tells you to buy a certain building in a certain location. The treasurer doesn't like that location, or perhaps his family built the first building and he refuses to release the funds and begins to be the one who brings division to the body. That is too far-fetched you say? I have dealt with it over and over in ministry after ministry helping people fix this very problem as well as having experienced it myself in my second church. You may be saying that your treasurer or the one you are thinking of is someone close to you that you trust. Maybe you are saying they are spiritual and you would never have that problem. My friend, may I enlighten you? Once spiritual does not mean always spiritual! I am not trying to imply that you cannot trust anyone but, you cannot trust anyone! You must realize that all men are frail. All have weaknesses. Those weaknesses will be tested.

This same problem can arise in any area of your ministry without proper structure and authority being set in place. It is not humble to give responsibility God has given you to others to prove that you can be trusted. This is a fallacy that many a minister has fallen into. God has counted you faithful by putting you into the ministry. You do not have to prove yourself faithful. Men will follow your lead if you are confident that God has called you and you are responsible for what God has called you to accomplish. Each man must give account of himself before God. If you are not God's servant according to Romans 14:4, you will not be able to stand.

If you are God's man or woman, God is able to make you stand. God is able to equip you and give you grace to carry out the responsibility He has appointed you. You are no different than Moses, or Joshua, God will enable you despite your own human frailties. After you have taken your place just as Moses did, then you will be able to appoint other faithful men who will answer to you. At the same time knowing your weaknesses will enable you to set up a structure of accountability and checks and balances that will guard you and keep you from sudden destruction.

The word of God tells us in Proverbs 3 that if we preserve sound judgment and discernment that we will have no fear of sudden disaster or of the ruin that overtakes the wicked, for the Lord will be our confidence and will keep our feet from being snared.

Let me give you something to consider. If you had a new born baby, would you just give that baby to someone to care for because they have been a parent before? Or would you let someone else care and discipline and nurture that child rather than yourself? I think not. Your vision and ministry in God's eyes is just as great a responsibility as raising a child. I am reminded of the scripture in Hebrews 13:17. "Obey your leaders and submit to their authority. They keep watch over you as men who must give an account. Obey them so that their work will be a joy, not a burden, for that would be of no advantage to you." You will give account for those whom God has entrusted to you and each person you delegate authority will not give the account only for their actions but you as their leader will because they are simply operating under delegate authority. In other words you are giving them the power to act in your stead, as your representative, as though you were doing the wielding of the muscle.

When we formulate By Laws we have to decide first where do we want the final decision to rest? Should it rest in a group of individual board members with a ¾ majority voting system? Should it rest on the vote of the congregation? Should it rest upon the visionary or the pastor? I think by now you know the direction I feel the authority should fall. Yes, upon the visionary. There are stipulations such as large expenditures and complete redirection that need to be approved by a large number of your supporters but there are very few items within a healthy church structure that people need to have a say in.

Did Moses ever ask the children of Israel their opinion about what decisions he should make? No, but they were quick to give them anyway. Do you know how many ministries have crumbled over chairs or pews? Over carpet! Or how about the church board that has the power to hold a meeting in your absence and votes that you are no longer the "right" man for the job around here? If you're By Laws allow it, in times of war like this your whole ministry may crumble. I hope you are getting a vivid picture now of the problems that often arise due to a lack of good structure.

One of the greatest weaknesses of a minister is that because of the grace upon their life, they are often to trusting of humans to do the right thing in all situations. There are however, some ministers who have abused the place of authority and don't welcome insight of others. There must be a balance in your leadership but when it comes down to where the final authority or governments are held it is vital to have those in the right place.

Many times church founders or charter members begin to think they are the ones who will decide the outcome of a ministry. After-all, they have been with this thing since the beginning. They have been faithful to tithe and attend they begin to form a democracy and begin trying to control a church with money or clout. Not church people! Yes, church people, a.k.a, Christians. When people are ready to take their seat they will begin to ask such questions as; "who decides this or that?" "Who do you answer to?" "Who is your covering?" "Don't we get to vote on this?" "I have been a faithful member, don't I have a say." That will be the day you will be very glad you have communicated to them the way we do it here is...... It will also be the day you will be very glad your house is in order.

I do not recommend appointment of ANY church members on your executive council of leaders but rather licensed and ordained ministers. From my own sad experiences I found that it was too hard for people in the church to make spiritual decisions about other people in the flock. There is a grace necessary to handle and to "separate" such matters. That grace is not given to a sheep it is given to shepherds. I have seen many wonderful people with wonderful intentions be caught in the cross fire of flesh verses spirit, family verses church membership, even spouses who are out of line. I have seen it almost virtually impossible for people to separate the act from the person they fellowship with in church. It in my opinion is too much to ask of a member. Though people "think" they can handle it. From experience I tell you, they cannot.

All that most people generally want from a ministry is a feeling of security, and confidence and trust in their leaders. They need to know how things are run so they can run with you. If this is well established in your map of objectives and By Laws then it will be very easy to win the confidence of your followers. If they see a balance of personal accountability it will bring a place of rest to their minds. But, if people ask them thing like; "don't you have a church board?" "Who makes the decisions at your church?" "Are you on the committee?" If your members don't know how things work they will be fearful or confused so at this stage, communication becomes a very important key to successful unity.

CHAPTER FIVE

HOW TO WRITE YOUR BY LAWS

People don't mind having a person in charge if they know that person is being held accountable and proven reliable. They also have to have confidence that their leader is going to follow the word way when handling problems and going to walk the love walk in every situation. It is time for us to get to the meat of the issue. Let's begin to break down the specific By Laws and what needs to be included in them.

I am going to break down each section of By Laws for the Local church in general and then following I will bring together a sample of how By Laws should be written as an example for you to follow. You may use these By Laws freely and take them as your own if you so desire. I have put them in this book to be of help to you and to your team to accomplish your goals for the Kingdom of heaven. You may have to revise some things based on your own convictions and tenants of faith of which we will cover in a later chapter.

The very first thing that must be defined in your By Laws is who the President of the organization may be. Most generally that would be the Pastor in Charge. Then you must begin by defining what is a Pastor and how does he/she qualify for that office. Also you will include his/her duties as the head and what he/she has the power to do. You will also include what will disqualify him/her as the authority. This gives way to remove someone from authority if they are not living according to the scriptural definition of that office. It is not about likes and dislikes of personality or leadership style but only disqualification that is laid out in scripture. We would call this section Article 1 with sections dividing the different responsibilities and requirements.

When you review this section you will see many things defined such as qualifications and responsibilities that are solely his/hers. You will also see that he/she is given access to handle funds if necessary or what he/she may delegate as deemed necessary. Included in this section will be what to do if a pastor loses his qualifications and how his/her position will be filled. Who will handle things when he/she is absent and where will authorization be delegated? Also defined will be those who will work with him/her as a governing body and what their limitation of power will be.

As you know this office of God is considered a Five-fold ministry gift of God according to Ephesians chapter 4. This is not an office to be entered into lightly or by human decision. This must be entered into only by divine calling and appointment. It is also an office that will guard and keep the flock of God. Souls entering the kingdom of God must be able to see one who is a leader or a shepherd as one who lives an astute life. Or another description as Paul reported it should be held by one who walks circumspectly.

Article 2 & 3 follow with the definition of Elders and Deacons. These positions can be handled too lightly and also to highly in most churches. It is my opinion that it should be years of testing the motives of individuals hearts before these offices are delegated. They should not be entered into lightly nor appointed without much discretion and proven spiritual maturity.

Most people want pastors to hand out these positions for the purpose of status or power to act. They should be offices that are entered into by invitation not request. I have come to find in my experience in today's world there are very few Christians who can hold these positions with great humility of heart and proper respect for the head of the church. This depends greatly upon the background of the people serving as well as the amount of proper teaching they receive from the head.

I have had the privilege of experiencing firsthand the proper scriptural role of both the deacon and the elder demonstrated to me in churches in other countries. Because of the infra-structure of American business or shall we call it westernization, there is an imbalance of power placed on these roles within the local church. In foreign lands however, I have seen these positions embodied in a sound scriptural form and with humble hearts by those who hold them. Men and women highly respected for their exemplary lives and service to others. They, coming alongside the man or woman of God leading them as true bondsmen and women to serve and to help their leader. They are not only held in high regard by all but their words carry holy weightiness due to their demonstration of love, respect and wisdom. Such humility and spiritual maturity are lacking today in the American home and the American church to our loss of a great treasure God has given to His local church. Many denominations make these appointments based on financial status, longest attendee, and length of salvation. None of which I feel are a scriptural basis for such positions. A deacon and an elder must have a full understanding of the price of Calvary. What is presented to God must first pass through death and is presented to be consumed by fire. The highest call is to die to oneself.

What is an Elder and what is a Deacon? Let us begin by defining these positions. An Elder should be co-adjudicators, that is to say a person who can make judgments together with the Pastor on serious spiritual matters and other decisions in the church. There are qualifications for such a position. For defining of protocol we must look to our standard. There is only one. It is the Word of God.

Here is a trustworthy saying: If anyone sets his heart on being an overseer, he desires a noble task. Now the overseer must be above reproach, the husband of but one wife, temperate, self-controlled, respectable, hospitable, able to teach, not given to drunkenness, not violent but gentle, not quarrelsome, not a lover of money. He must manage his own family well and see that his children obey him with proper respect. (If anyone does not know how to manage his own family, how can he take care of God's church?) He must not be a recent convert, or he may become conceited and fall under the same judgment as the devil. He must also have a good reputation with outsiders, so that he will not fall into disgrace and into the devil's trap. (1 Timothy 3:1-7 NIV) These are not just suggestions they are God's way of doing things. Now one particular statement I wish to address that has been taken completely out of context on many occasions and has cost churches dearly is the statement, "husband of one wife." Many churches teach that if someone has ever been divorced he cannot qualify to be an elder. However in the time this was written Polygamy was a very huge problem among the newly converted and caused much controversy in the churches and much confusion as well. So Paul as an Apostle was establishing guidelines and doctrine to help the church to redefine marriage and what marriage should be to the Christian. He was not talking about that a man should never remarry or that divorce was an unpardonable sin as some churches reflect. Rather he was stating that an Elder should not have more than one wife. However, it is very commendable for one to be in a marriage and that that union be one that lasts forever as God truly designed marriage to be. But we should not forget that God does forgive and people are usable who have failed marriages. However they should have a stable home life and good marriage as well.

Now for our second scripture: An elder must be blameless, the husband of but one wife, a man whose children believe and are not open to the charge of being wild and disobedient. Since an overseer is entrusted with God's work, he must be blameless-- not overbearing, not quick-tempered, not given to drunkenness, not violent, not pursuing dishonest gain. Rather he must be hospitable, one who loves what is good, who is self-controlled, upright, holy and disciplined. He must hold firmly to the trustworthy message as it has been taught, so that he can encourage others by sound doctrine and refute those who oppose it. (Titus 1:6-9 NIV)

There are some very clear definitions as to the character of one who will handle spiritual decisions in the church and they should not be ignored. There too are responsibilities that an elder should be aware of. From Miletus, Paul sent to Ephesus for the elders of the church. (Acts 20:17 NIV)

Keep watch over yourselves and all the flock of which the Holy Spirit has made you overseers. Be shepherds of the church of God, which he bought with his own blood. (Acts 20:28 NIV)

In everything I did, I showed you that by this kind of hard work we must help the weak, remembering the words the Lord Jesus himself said: 'It is more blessed to give than to receive.'" (Acts 20:35 NIV)

To visit the sick and pray for them as called upon. And the prayer offered in faith will make the sick person well; the Lord will raise him up. If he has sinned, he will be forgiven. (James 5:15 NIV)

Also remember this: Whoever turns a sinner from the error of his way will save him from death and cover over a multitude of sins. (James 5:20 NIV)

Religion that God our Father accepts as pure and faultless is this: to look after orphans and widows in their distress and to keep oneself from being polluted by the world. (James 1:27 NIV)

Not only should these guideline be adhered to but in this article divided in sections, should be defined how such a person should be appointed, for how long as well. Also the failure to fulfill his given responsibility or should he no longer remain qualified how should he be removed.

I also recommend that you would ask a person to serve on a yearly appointed term not that it cannot be renewed however, that way if there are problems that arise or difficulties for that person in service there is an end and point of closure rather that someone being appointed life time and then the Pastors finds their heart and desire is not pure and has not recourse except critical measures to release the brother.

Next we move on to defining the role of a Deacon. Again we look to the scriptures as our guide.

In those days when the number of disciples was increasing, the Grecian Jews among them complained against the Hebraic Jews because their widows were being overlooked in the daily distribution of food. So the Twelve gathered all the disciples together and said, "It would not be right for us to neglect the ministry of the word of God in order to wait on tables. Brothers, choose seven men from among you who are known to be full of the Spirit and wisdom. We will turn this responsibility over to them and will give our attention to prayer and the ministry of the word." This proposal pleased the whole group. They chose Stephen, a man full of faith and of the Holy Spirit; also Philip, Procorus, Nicanor, Timon, Parmenas, and Nicolas from Antioch, a convert to Judaism. They presented these men to the apostles, who prayed and laid their hands on them. So the word of God spread. The number of disciples in

Jerusalem increased rapidly, and a large number of priests became obedient to the faith. (Acts 6:1-7 NIV)

The deacons shall assist in the temporal matters of the church as directed by the Pastor and Elders. How must they qualify? Brothers, choose seven men from among you who are known to be full of the Spirit and wisdom. We will turn this responsibility over to them (Acts 6:3 NIV)

Deacons, likewise, are to be men worthy of respect, sincere, not indulging in much wine, and not pursuing dishonest gain. They must keep hold of the deep truths of the faith with a clear conscience. They must first be tested; and then if there is nothing against them, let them serve as deacons. In the same way, their wives are to be women worthy of respect, not malicious talkers but temperate and trustworthy in everything. A deacon must be the husband of but one wife and must manage his children and his household well. Those who have served well gain an excellent standing and great assurance in their faith in Christ Jesus. (1 Timothy 3:8-13 NIV)

These scriptures clearly define what kind of member of your church is fit for such an office.

Do not be hasty in the laying on of hands, and do not share in the sins of others. Keep yourself pure. (1 Timothy 5:22 NIV)

This verse I think proves to be an important one concerning Elders and Deacons. These are not just titles and positions to be taken lightly and tossed around as tools for promotion. They are positions if not held in reverence and high regard will destroy a body of believers. It may take a Pastor as many as six long years to find qualified men and women to fill such positions with in the church. You must really know people well and in today's society the slower the better at these appointments. I have seen many churches greatly damaged because a Pastor was coerced or even pressured to make these appointments and when done prematurely have cost these ministries dearly. It takes time to really know if someone lives a life above reproach. I believe that we as leaders will be held accountable not only for our own lives but for the power we give to others in our stead. We must weigh each man's heart and motive seriously. However, even doing so may result in wrong appointments. Someone may start out with the right heart but be poisoned and become disqualified and for the sake of the body must be quickly removed. Remember our members are entrusted to us by the Lord and for their lives we will give account to our heavenly father. I cannot caution you enough to not get in a hurry or be pressured by men but be led by God.

We will move on now to Article 4. This Article will define how meetings will be conducted and how they will be scheduled and who will preside over those meetings and who will attend them. We may feel these things to be petty and unnecessary but remember we are writing them not for law but for guidance in times of war not peace. These must be clearly stated so that things can be done decently and in order.

Article 5 Will go on to state how elections of these positions will be done, who will make the said appointments to these positions and how long of terms they will serve. Again this is a protective mechanism for the health of all involved as well as to provide order to the structure.

Before I progress further in our bylaws below I want to provide to you the ramifications of what has been discussed so far. These are an example of how to write up these articles for your benefit. Remember that this is a guideline for you and it is best if once compiled according to your taste that you have a tax exempt lawyer review them.

ARTICLE I

PASTOR/ LOCAL CHURCH PRESBYTERY

SECTION 1:

PASTOR

He/She must be divinely called by God to feed and have the oversight of His flock; having prepared himself for, and proven faithful to the ministry for such a period of time as the Church deems necessary.

SECTION 2:

He/ She must qualify to hold this ministerial office according to 1 Timothy 3:1-7; Titus 1:5-9.

SECTION 3:

He/She must be born again by the Spirit of God and living in the experience, John 3:5-6.

SECTION 4:

He/She must be baptized in water by immersion after he is a believer, according to Matthew 28:19, Acts 2:38-41

SECTION 5:

He/She must be baptized with the Holy Spirit according to Acts 2:4,6:5,9:17, Luke 4:18; John 7:38,39.

SECTION 6:

He must have a divine call to the ministry. Acts 9:15, 13:31, Ephesians 4:11.

SECTION 7:

A Pastor is required by God to feed the flock, John 21:15-17; to take the oversight of the Church, 1 Peter 5:2,3; he shall visit the members of the household of faith, James 1:27.

SECTION 8:

The Pastor is the presiding chairman at all the Church business meetings and team meetings, Acts 21:17-18; 15:13-21. These scriptures indicate that James was the Pastor of the Church in

Jerusalem and that he was the presiding chairman of the meetings of the Elders and later at the Assembly business meeting. Acts 15:22.

SECTION 9:

The Pastor, (presiding chairman), alone can call a special Church business meeting. No one else has this authority without the Pastor's approval.

SECTION 10:

The Pastor has power to appoint any Trustee to act as Chairman of the Presbytery meetings and Church business meetings in the event of his absence.

SECTION 11:

In the event the Church should be without a Pastor, or if the Pastor should loose his Scriptural qualification to remain in office, the Local Church Presbytery may call a special Church business meeting for the purpose of directing the affairs of the Church.

SECTION 12:

LOCAL CHURCH GOVERNING STRUCTURE:

Local church Presbytery is comprised of 4 Ordained Ministers
of the Gospel to set on this Council along with and appointed by
the resident Pastor, also seated as non-voting members may be
the and Secretary and Treasurer of the church. For financial
decisions, a finance advisory team may also be set up by the
appointment of the Pastor.

The only body holding any governing or voting
decisions of the church is the local Presbytery. The other
councils will only hold the power to advise and give
recommendation and counsel to the Presbytery when called
upon by any two members of the Presbytery to do so.
The Presbytery will work alongside the local Pastor to
determine any legal or spiritual matters that must be attended to
that are beyond the Pastor's individual ability.

SECTION 13:

The Pastor shall be co-depositor with the Trustee of the Church
(the Trustee shall be an appointed elder who is a member of the
congregation) of all funds of the Church and shall sign all
disbursements, together with the Trustee or any other Local
Presbytery member that is authorized for signature. All
disbursements should be discussed and approved by the Local
Church Presbytery that are outside of the general expenditures
of the Local Church and ministry such as the purchase of land,
mortgages or any substantial financial endeavor.

SECTION 14:

In the event of the disability or absence of the Secretary or Trustee, the Pastor shall have the power to delegate power temporarily to another officer of the Church during the disability or absence of the Trustee or Secretary.

SECTION 15:

In the event of the vacancy of the Pastorate, the Local Church Presbytery of said church will be welcomed to submit recommendations of candidates for approval. The Local Church Presbytery which has the Pastoral vacancy will come together with a committee comprised of five tithe paying members of the present congregation who will be chosen by the Presbytery for the purpose of appointment of a new Pastor. This joint group must have a 3/4 vote to approve a new Pastor. Any vacating Pastor, who leaving in good standing at the discretion of the Presbytery, may be included in these meetings and also submit recommendations for a candidate to this special Committee with equal part and involvement and voting power in this appointment process.

SECTION 16:

Any or all Pastors must maintain current Credentials with the _____ ORG and may in addition hold credentials with another an organization of its Presbytery member's organization or another reputable ministry in good standing with the Presbytery. They must remain up to date on all annual fees. Credentials may be held with other organizations as well, but one must remain in good standing with the Presbytery of the Church and comply with the doctrine of the church in which they Pastor. Failure to remain in good standing with LWCC organization will result in disqualification to remain the Pastor/President of this Church.

ARTICLE 2

RESIDENT ELDER

SECTION 1:

Elders are the attendant ministers or subordinate - co-adjudicators of the Pastor and other Elders. Acts 6:1-7. They shall assist in spiritual matters of the Church as called upon by Pastor and the Local Presbytery. A local resident elder must qualify in accordance to 1Timothy 3:1-7; Titus 1:6–9. He shall assist the Pastor (who is presiding or chief elder) in all spiritual matters concerning the oversight of the Church at the Pastors request. Acts 20:17,28,35; to visit the sick and pray for them as called upon by members, James 5:14,15; visit the widows and fatherless in their afflictions, James 1:27; etc.

SECTION 2:

Failure on an Elder's part to remain qualified as stated in Section 1 of this Article is cause for removal from the office of an Elder by the Local Presbytery or Pastor, as deemed necessary. This removal may be publicly announced to the congregation if deemed necessary by the Pastor or the Local Presbytery.

SECTION 3:

The appointment and installation of Elders will be conducted publicly as necessary after the candidate has been by the accepted and by the agreement of the Presbytery. One or more members of the Presbytery shall conduct public installation. The Local Presbytery and members of the Local Church body may submit recommendations for consideration for possible appointments to the Pastor. A form of recommendation for local Elders must be submitted to the Pastor for evaluation and approval. A formal installation should be held before the congregation at inception of this process by the Pastor of the Organization to insure proper understanding to the church of the process of delegation in the local church and the proper definition of the said appointment. The Pastor may make these appointments on an annual basis.

ARTICLE 3

DEACONS

SECTION 1:

Deacons are the attendant ministers or subordinate-co-adjudicators of the Pastor and the Elders.   Acts 6:1-7. They shall assist in all temporal matters of the Church as directed by the Pastor and Elders.

SECTION 2:

They must qualify in accordance to Acts 6:3, 1 Tim. 3:8-13.

SECTION 3:

They must be members in good standing of the Local church and also have a good report with those who are outside the Church.

SECTION 4:

Failure to remain qualified as stated in this section will be grounds for immediate removal by the Pastor or Local Church Presbytery.

ARTICLE 4

MEETINGS:

SECTION 1:

The Pastor and Presbytery shall first discuss all-important Church matters. Upon approval they may, if they so desire, present it to the Church elders, deacons and congregation however, final decisions are to be made by the Presbytery.

SECTION 2:

An annual Church business meeting shall be held at a given time chosen by the President/ Pastor during the month of February after the closing of each fiscal year. This annual Church business meeting may be waived by a 2/3 vote of the Local Church Presbytery and notification given to the congregation, and rescheduled for accounting delays. However, financial statements are to be submitted annually to any tithing member. Individual contribution reports shall be prepared each January for the previous fiscal year, examined for accuracy, and distributed by the fourth Sunday in January to all contributors of $100.00 and above.

ARTICLE 5

SECTION 1:

The Pastor of the Church cannot be removed from any office held in any local church for their lifetime except for moral reasons and then only with a 3/4-majority vote of the members of the local Presbytery.

SECTION 2:

The Elders agreed upon by the Local Presbytery will be appointed by and installed by the Pastor, Acts 14:23; Titus 1:5. They shall hold office as long as they remain scripturally qualified, hold fast to the vision of the Church, or until such time when they voluntarily resign the office. They may also be removed due to the Pastor's discretion with the agreement of the Presbytery.

SECTION 3:

Deacons are nominated and elected by the Local Pastor and Elders and Presbytery and or present Elders and their term of office shall be annually, at which time they can be reinstated by approval of the Presbytery.

CHAPTER SIX

ARTICLES 6-10
MEMBERSHIP, DISCIPLINE& GOVERNMENTS

In this chapter we will discuss the three following items: Membership, Church Discipline, and Governments. These three areas are very meaty issues. Beginning with Article 6 we will determine in this section who is a qualified member of this ministry and we will also define his/her powers and duties. Each entity established will have its own ideas as to how people will be taken in as members. This must be well defined in your By Laws so that there is no discrepancy when it comes to legal matters of the church. You must also define how a member is not only qualified but disqualified. In the area of discipline as well which you will find in Article 7, you must broadly define how matters dealing with members will be settled. You must also list who will decide these matters and how they will be settled. As you will note there is very little detail given here but enough I feel, to *cover the bases*.

Article 8 deals with the governments and will become more detailed and fragmented based on each person's responsibility. As you will see a legal governor of the organization will be appointed in this section. I have written it as I have written previously as the Pastor being the head. You may however, have another philosophy of leadership such as a committee or a plurality of leadership of which I also have address and voiced my views. Whatever your preference, this is the article to which your decision is assigned. In other words, to whom is the power vested. There are items of protocol such as sacraments of the church will also be listed here and that the church has the power to uphold those sacraments. Communion, baptism, confirmations, baby dedication can all be put in this section. We only saw it necessary to list communion here.

In section 3 of Article 8 control of property is listed and to who ecclesiastical power and authority will be given. You will never understand how important this section is unless you have to face property battles due to church splits or other such hindrances to building the kingdom of God. In section 4 we talk about how salaries will be handled. As the Pastor is given charge of the ministry this is an area that you must place a guideline of protection for him/her that his personal salary will be set by an outside source. My recommendation is that of a ministerial group of people who have a heart for the needs of a Pastor as well as understanding of the time given to the work. It also provides a safeguard that protects the Pastor from those who may want to have power to control him/her by squeezing the dollars to take political advantage of the man or woman of God assigned to the local ministry. It is very difficult to find any group of people within the church who can handle such matters with excellence and nondiscrimination. This provides a healthy set of checks and balances for the minister and the congregation. There are also other things the IRS likes such as the comparison of salaries to others in the same size town and congregation. Such surveys are available to be viewed before a legitimate salary is established for the minister in charge as well as the leaders under him/her.

In Section 5 we must establish that no monies will be given to those who govern the church unless they are paid employees of the ministry in other areas. They will however receive no renumeration for setting on the Presbytery. In section 6 of this article it will be stated how often this governing entity must meet. Section 7 establishes the fiscal calendar which is another aspect of government. The last section in Article 8 will be the way a member will be disqualified from membership status.

Moving on now to Article 9 where we will see the definition of church secretary and treasurer. Here each section will define things such as role, appointment procedure, length of office if so desired. I have left this out due to the fact that I want the liberty to remove anyone that is not compliant at any time and not be restricted by time frames. Also responsibilities will be defined, how vacancies will be filled.

Article 10 deals in more detail with membership and who has voting power. You must also define inactive membership and loss of voting power. You may feel that this too in unnecessary. It is very necessary. I have had a personal experience that prompted this section to be written.

In the first church where my husband and I were Pastoring, we took over a preexisting work with many problems in leadership. The situation got very much out of hand due to some very unruly and irremovable board members. These board members decided to hold a congregational meeting to dismiss out without our knowledge and had the power to do so due to faulty By Laws. They also had the power to call anyone a member they so chose to because membership was also not clearly defined. This created a membership of 300 people of which only about 70 truly were people who still were in attendance and financially contributed to the local church there. We did however find out about the meeting and publicly resigned instead of dealing any longer with insubordinate leadership. We had poured our hearts and lives into many people for 18 months but due to what we inherited, we had to walk away from it all with nothing but the clothes on our backs. It was a very disturbing situation of which only God could rectify in our own lives personally. From that point in our ministry in the future, we clearly defined these matters before taking positions or when formulating guidelines, policies and by laws.

Below you will find these two articles and how they might be written.

ARTICLE 9

SECRETARY AND TREASURE OF THIS LOCAL CHURCH

SECTION 1:

SECRETARY:

A Trustee of the Local Presbytery shall be acting Secretary of the Presbytery and shall be appointed by the Pastor and sanctioned by the Presbytery.

SECTION 2:

The secretary's duties shall be to keep the custody of the Seal, and shall keep a complete record of all minutes of all church business.

SECTION 3:

TREASURER:

The treasurer shall be a trustee or any member of the Local Church Presbytery and shall be appointed by the Pastor and sanctioned by the Local Presbytery.

SECTION 4:

The appointed Trustee of the Local Church shall be entrusted with the finances of the Church in the following manner. He/She shall keep an itemized account of all the receipts and disbursements of all monies received. He/she shall submit an itemized report quarterly concerning the financial activities to Advisory Council of the churches and to the Director of Finance of the Presbytery who will record account activity. The Trustee shall upon request submit them to the Finance Team if one has been appointed by the Pastor and the Presbytery for review. He/she shall make a complete summarized statement at the annual business meeting of the church. He/she shall make all disbursements under the oversight of the local Pastor. He/ she shall deposit all funds in the name of the Church, in a responsible bank designated by the Pastor.

SECTION 5:

VACANCIES:

In the event of a vacancy the Pastor may appoint a new member immediately to the Presbytery upon their 2//3 approval for replacement.

ARTICLE 10

VOTING MEMBERSHIP:

SECTION 1:

ACTIVE MEMBERS:

17 years of age and older constitute the voting constituency of the Local Church provided they have met the qualifications of an active member by following the procedures set for in the local church.

SECTION 2:

INACTIVE MEMBERS:

Members who shall without good reason be absent themselves from the services of the Church for a period of two consecutive months or more; who cease to contribute of their means to its financial support, by way of tithes and offerings; who may be out of harmony with its teachings or its ministries; who shall be under charge for misconduct; or who may have fallen under condemnation through sinful or worldly practices outside of the teachings of the Bible, shall be considered inactive members and shall lose their right to vote until restored in good standing upon approval by the Presbytery of each local assembly to which they are a member.

AMENDMENTS AND QUORUM

We will look now into the next two articles of the By Laws. Articles 11 &12 discuss these two words: amendments and quorum. These two must be clearly defined before we go any further. An amendment is a correction or a reform or improvement into a new era or a situation that presents the need to alter the present procedures. For example you may have a change in the structure or flow of an organization or a resignation of a key leader or director of your organization. At this point an amendment may need to be made as to how decisions will be made when you consider the best interest of the organization or the people involved. Second, we have the word Quorum. A quorum is the minimum number of members of an assembly or an organization that must be present at a meeting to make the proceedings valid. This section too is important to have in your bylaws too because of what we stated earlier, times of war. In times of war people who don't have things go their way can cause an uprising of others to come against the leadership. If they themselves are leaders you want to protect the organization from decrementing due to the foolish decisions of an angry person with influence. In other words no one would have the power to just come tear down what you have built with a "meeting" of those who were on their side of the matter. Many a Pastor have been voted out of their pulpits due to this one thing being left out of the by laws because it defines how a decision is determined to be valid. Validity is very important in negative situations. It is also important in positive situations to prove to a congregation you have the support of others for instance in a building program.

These articles can be written very simply stated as follows:

ARTICLE 11

AMENDMENTS:

SECTION 1:

A duly called meeting of the Presbytery may make amendments to this constitution. Amendment(s) may be made by a two-thirds majority vote of the members present and voting, providing the members present form a quorum.

ARTICLE 12

QUORUM

No meeting shall be considered as an official or special business meeting of the Assembly unless two-thirds or more of the voting members shall be present to constitute a quorum; and then only on permission of the Pastor/President of the Local Church Body.

That will conclude this section of governmental issues. In the next chapter we will cover articles 13& 14 dealing with ministerial issues for your organization.

CHAPTER 7

CREDENTIALS AND HOLY ORDINANCES

In this chapter we will discuss the contents of Article 13 and 14. One thing you have to remember about By Laws is that it is a guideline defining what and how things will be instituted. You must also remember there will be time when you wish to UN-appoint something or someone that has been instated. To do this you must also have provision in your By Laws that tells how you will be able to undo something that has been done.

This is very important when it comes to giving credentials. To me Ministerial Credentials are not something to be taken lightly. Though they have been handed out without any reverence by many organizations for just a fee or service, I don't believe that is how they were originally handled. Just as any other profession in society I believe that one should be approved and proven to be fit to be a member of such a high office. After all this office is God given not man installed. Many people forget that. Because of my beliefs you will find details that reflect my convictions in this matter. You will find very clear guidelines concerning not only credentials but renewal and fees.

According to the Word of God, as a minister you will be held accountable for the lives of the persons that are entrusted to you. Heb 13:17 (NIV) "Obey your leaders and submit to their authority. They keep watch over you as men who must give an account. Obey them so that their work will be a joy, not a burden, for that would be of no advantage to you."

Here are two other important scriptures to consider one is 1 Peter 4:10-11(NIV)"Each one should use whatever gift he has received to serve others, faithfully administering God's grace in its various forms. If anyone speaks, he should do it as one speaking the very words of God. If anyone serves, he should do it with the strength God provides, so that in all things God may be praised through Jesus Christ. To him be the glory and the power for ever and ever. Amen"

And 1Peter 5:2-4 (NIV) "Be shepherds of God's flock that is under your care, serving as overseers-- not because you must, but because you are willing, as God wants you to be; not greedy for money, but eager to serve; not lording it over those entrusted to you, but being examples to the flock. And when the Chief Shepherd appears, you will receive the crown of glory that will never fade away."

Guarding and guiding a flock is to be taken seriously before God and men. Unfortunately because of the abuse of this God ordained office, demoralization and lack of respect have been given as do people now tend to disrespect any figure of authority in this day from the highest authority down. We cannot change what has happened or what is but we can strengthen what remains and make our regulations one that stand against immorality and the breakdown of moral standards.

Sections 2, 3, &4 state just what those credentials give a Minister the power to do within your organization. The revoking of Credentials is then stated in Section 5. We go from there on to Article 14 where some sacraments are named and defined. The five that our particular organization deem as necessary to be listed and defined are Baptism, Dedication, Communion and Marriage and Ordination. Here are examples of Articles 13, 14 respectively.

ARTICLE 13

MINISTERIAL CREDENTIALS

SECTION 1:

CREDENTIALS:

A candidate for ministry Credentials must request the appropriate application to apply for license or ordination with _____ Church. All paperwork, must be submitted and to the Presbytery and Advisor Council of the fellowship of churches along with a recommendation from the Pastor and referral forms, (unseen by candidate), must also be returned to the Presbytery and application fee of $100.00 must be received before consideration and acceptance for Credentials and ministerial position can be approved. If approved by the Presbytery and the Advisory Council the local church may license the said candidate with annual renewals pending for the first five years. Following those five years the said Councils may give permanent ordination if candidate has remained in good standing however, retain the right to continue on a year by year renewal for as long as they deem necessary.

SUBSECTION 1:

CERTIFICATES:

This church shall issue to each candidate a Gospel Ministry license or a Certificate of Ordination which shall verify that such person has been licensed or ordained according to the by law as of this Church, bearing also the date and place where the ceremony was performed, tighter with the signature of the Pastor and all appointed governing elders and having the official church seal affixed thereto.

SUBSECTION 2:

INDENTIFICATION CARD:

This church shall also issue to each approved candidate an Identification Card which shall verify that such person is in good standing with this Church, according to its bylaws, said Identification card to be renewable annually.

SUBSECTION 3:

FEES AND DUES:

No fees or dues shall be assessed by this Church for license or ordination after initial application fee of any person to Gospel ministry, by virtue of the conscientious religious belief held by the founder and by the Advisory council that such ceremony is only the human acknowledgment of God's holy investiture which has, by diving sovereignty, already taken place (mark 3:14; John 15:16) and that since true ministerial authority is bestowed by God through his infinite grace, therefore this Church shall not assess or otherwise require fees or dues for its official recognition of such a divine commission.

SECTION 2:

A minister in good standing which is licensed or ordained by _____ Church shall be granted the full privileges of performing marriage ceremonies; conducting baptisms; serving communion; conducting funerals; permission granted for access to hospitals, jails, prisons, etc; providing appropriate spiritual counseling; and other full ministerial privileges as required.

SECTION 3:

A Minster of _____ Church shall
only have the right to marry in accordance with Holy Scriptures
as defined and handed down as policy from the Pastor and the
Constitution and By- Laws.

SECTION 4:

Credentials must be renewed annually until released in good
conscience by the Advisory Council. The purpose of this
practice is in order to assure that each licensed or ordained
minister is remaining true to his call, being faithful to perform in
his/her call, living above reproach, continuing to remain
accountable for their life and ministry decisions and that they
are bearing the fruit deemed required by a minister of the gospel
and the fees for the furtherance of the Gospel.

SECTION 5:

REVOCATION OF CREDENTIALS:

a.)   Ordination, License to Minister of Christian Worker's
       Certificate may be revoked by the Advisory Council upon
       Substantiation of gross moral charges, serious departure
       from faith, or manifest acts or rebellion against the
       Church.

b.) Such Certificates or Licenses remain the property of the Church. In regards to revocation of such assessments, see Article 24 of these by- laws.

ARTICLE 14

SACRAMENTS

SECTION 1:

BAPTISM:

Water baptism will be by full immersion, except when not possible due to any medical reason. Baptism will be preformed upon the request of the candidate and will serve as an outward sign and testimony of the believer and their decision to follow Christ.

SECTION 2:

DEDICATION:

Dedication is available for all parents who desire to "present their infants to the Lord" Dedication will also include the charge to the parents to raise the children in line with Biblical principles. We will not water baptize infants.

SECTION 3:

COMMUNION:

Communion will be served as often as is consistent with good practice, but will not be allowed to become a weekly or monthly ritual. Communion will be open to all believers present, the one and only requirement is that the individual claims to be "born-again" Christian according to Romans 10:9, 10.

SECTION 4:

MARRIAGE;

A licensed or ordained minister will perform marriages. This organization will only recognize the union of one man and one woman in Holy Matrimony to constitute, that which is sacred and acceptable in the sight of God. This organization does not permit the union of same sex or trans-sexual unions.

SECTION 5:

ORDINATION:

Ordination will be performed for anyone having proved their divine gift and calling to the ministry of the Gospel of Jesus Christ and so desiring Ordination. This certification will only be given after the Presbytery and Pastor have followed the procedures set forth in the application for ordination. This ordination may be bestowed both publicly and privately. All candidates whom ordination is conferred upon shall have the rights and privileges of an ordained minister including the authority to solemnize marriages, conduct baptisms, burials and any other forms of religious worship and sacerdotal functions of the ministry. This recognition is available to both men and women who have proven their calling.

If you notice closely section four is clearly defined due to the gross misrepresentation of marriage in our world today. This belief it has been advised to me, should also be stated very clearly in your tenants of faith as these are what will truly stand up in the time of war concerning any discrimination matters in the court of the land. Therefore, we have put them in both places for our protection not to have to override our conviction of scripture due to equal rights and other such distortions of the truth in today's immoral society.

In this area of your By Laws I pray that you will take time to clarify everything that you must that conveys your convictions on all these matters of the clergy. When doing this, be sure to take note of all the abuses. Think of the person who is very zealous yet has no training and what licensing that person could cause in the lives of innocent individuals if given authority to guide people or counsel people before they are fully mature. It is more serious than you may think. As a leader people who have much zeal have always pulled on my heart. They are like Peter who wanted so much to follow Jesus but often took his eyes off of Jesus when it really mattered most. Yet, Jesus patiently taught and trained Peter and he became a great apostle once he was mature. Some leaders become pressured into selling licenses to people to build their base bigger. Others do it to build their own name and so that they can say to others that they have 100 ministers under their leadership.

In actuality however, these ministers do not even know the candidates that they have given credentials to and are not responsible for the actions of those who are conducting "ministry" and ruining lives. Let me ask you a question. "Is it wrong to expect the best out of people who will lead people?" I think not. It is best if you give someone a license first explaining to those to whom it is given it is a vehicle in which to prove their true calling. I think of the time Jesus appointed the 12 disciples power while he was still there with them. Give them a reasonable amount of time to test their calling and character, when they have truly proven their ministry, ordain them.

CHAPTER EIGHT

SOME BASIC THINGS IN ARTICLES 15-21

In this Chapter, I would like to point out some basic things that must be included in your By Laws. Some may seem to be repetitive or even unnecessary but they are restating within your By Laws some things that are in your original Articles and stated more clearly here. Most of them are legal in nature and are here for legal purposes mainly. Where you will be located, members, objectives, holding of property and nondiscrimination based on government policy will be found in Article 15. Article 16 will denote that you accept the doctrine of the Bible both Old and New Testaments in theory and practice and will personally acknowledge Jesus Christ as Savior and Lord and that those agreeing to these things will be able to become a member of the organization. Article 17 will restate the objectives of the ministry in paragraph form. Article 18 states how the management of the ministry will run and who will be given authority this should be only one paragraph. Article 19 will reiterate Property rights as found in the Articles of Incorporation, the hold of property, alienation of property, and certification of property. This should be written in three different sections. Article 20 will include a dissolution clause as to the dispersing of property should the ministry fold and how it will be divided to other nonprofit organizations. Article 21 will be called the Nondiscriminatory policy and will have vernacular that will state that in no way will this organization discriminate based on race, color, national or ethnic origin or the physically handicapped.

They are self-explanatory as follows:

ARTICLE 15:

NAME AND PLACE OF BUSINESS

The name by which this Local Church shall be known is _____. The principal place of business is located in the city of _____ in the state of_____.

ARTICLE 16:

MEMBERSHIP

Any person accepting the Doctrine of the Bible, Old and New Testaments in Theory and in practice and has personally acknowledge Jesus Christ as Savior and Lord may become a member by complying with the requirements relating to membership set forth in the Local Church.

ARTICLE 17:

OBJECTIVES

The objectives for which this Local Church is formed shall be: to preach and expound the Gospel of Jesus Christ according to the Holy Scriptures to educate and lead the people in the ways of salvation, goodness, righteousness, morality and temperance as taught in the bible. The prosecution of any religious, missionary, educational or charitable enterprise; it shall have the right to possess, buy, mortgage, sell, lease, barter and exchange real and personal property, to borrow money, collect funds, receive gifts and legacies as it may judge necessary for the attainment of theses objects. It shall have the power to license and ordain and send forth any missionary or preacher who has proven over a necessary period of time his divine gift and calling of God, to the satisfaction and approval of the Pastor, and Advisory Council and with the sanction of the Local Presbytery, Acts 15:22, each candidate must qualify scripturally according to 1 Timothy 3:1-7; Titus 1:5-9.

Each Church associated with this organization may inquire and apply for becoming an Extension Campus _____Bible Institute. Full consideration will then be given to the School Board of _____Bible Institute in conjunction with the Advisory Council to

_____Church's fellowship of churches for approval or disapproval.

ARTICLE 18:

MANAGEMENT

The management of this Local Church organization, spiritual, religious, educational and temporal, shall rest in its Pastor and Presbytery of the Local Assembly. Any vacancy in office shall be filled according to the procedure set forth in the Local Church By Laws.

ARTICLE 19:

PROPERTY RIGHTS

SECTION 1.

HOLDING OF PROPERTY

All property, real or chattel, shall be taken, held, sold, transferred, leased, rented, mortgaged, or conveyed in the Corporate name of the Local Church and submitted in writing for approval to the Local Church Presbytery for final approval to enter contracts and agreements will rest in this Local Church Government

SECTION 2.

ALINEATION OF PROPERTY:

No real property of the Church shall be sold, leased, rented, mortgaged or otherwise alienated unless the same shall have been authorized by at least a two-thirds majority vote of the Local Church Presbytery.

SECTION 3.

CERTIFICATION OF PROPERTY:

No less than two members of the Presbytery of this local church shall certify in such conveyance, lease, rental, or mortgage that the Presbytery has duly authored the same. Such certificates shall be held to be conclusive evidence thereof.

ARTICLE 20:

DISSOLUTION

This Local Church is organized pursuant to the general non-profit corporation laws. The property of this Local Church organization is irrevocably dedicated to religious, educational, and charitable purposes, and upon liquidation, dissolution or abandonment, after all financial liabilities have been paid in full, all the assets shall under the direction of the Local Presbytery

and may only be distributed to any organizations, foundation or fund, organized and operated for religious, educational, or charitable purposes and qualified for tax exemption purposes according to the Federal tax exemption code of the IRS.
No private person, individual member of the church or group shall be entitled to any part of the net earnings, properties or assets of the church in dissolution or otherwise. On liquidation or dissolution, all properties and assets of the church remaining after paying or providing for all debts and obligations shall be distributed to any 501 C 3 foundation, charitable or religious organizations with objectives viewed to be valid and in good standing with this local church

ARTICLE 21:

NONDISCRIMINATORY POLICY

The _____, does not discriminate on the basis of race, color, national and ethnic origin in administration of its Church, Schools, and all other Ministry activities.

Administration policies, scholarship and loan programs, and athletic and other school, Church, and various ministry programs will never be discriminatory but equal rights according to the Word of God will always be practiced by the_____.

CHAPTER NINE

FINANCE

Article 22 deals with Finance. In this section you will spell out the way in wish you will handle your accounting from who will make reports and to whom they will be reported to. There will also be shown how monies will be handled, offerings will be taken and counted. This process is very important and should be clearly spelled out to avoid shipwreck. Not included in this sample document are policies and procedures for finances. Since each ministry is distinctly different in its flow of funds and its daily operations these must be structured by you the director in a way that works for your people. However, policies should be discussed, documents and followed to insure excellence.

You can make a separate policy and procedure manual or you can insert it into this document under its own section of Article 22. If ever dealing with someone regarding embezzlement this would be a precious document in the court of law and should be read and signed by all who will handle funds of the corporation to be read and agreed to. There are detailed documents that you can find online to assist you in how to create such policies and guidelines. These form directives that leave little room for foul play or error. Providing, "checks and balances" as one may coin them.

In the second section of Article 22 you will find remuneration and allowances. These are guidelines and again directives as to who will decide what concerning reimbursement and payments, salaries and status of employees. Also listed here will be how the organization will obtain finances. I present to you a sample of this Article.

ARTICLE 22:

FINANCE

SECTION 1:

ACCOUNTING:

A. The director of finance shall be the president of the corporation or appointed by the Pastor and shall work in cooperation with the local presbytery and the Advisory Council in financial reporting.

B. The Local Presbytery shall have power to monitor these activities to ensure their efficient discharge. The receiving of financial reports can do this efficiently from the local church.

C. No local church member/ Pastor or Evangelist shall collect funds or offerings in the church for his personal purpose except so authorized at the time of collection by the Local Presbytery.

D. There shall be no private or hidden funds help by anyone or group or persons in the church or in the name of the church outside this particular local church without the knowledge and approval of the pastor, who will inform the Local Presbytery accordingly.

E. An accounting program, table of accounts, annual reports shall be prepared and its use enforced. A quarterly accounting report shall be presented to the Local Presbytery as well as the Advisory Council for review.

SECTION 2:

RENUMERATION AND ALLOWANCE :

A. 1 Corinthians 9:13, 14 shall apply here. However, the local Presbytery with the help of the Advisory Council shall determine from time to time what allowances shall be paid the Ministers of the Church. The Local Presbytery shall determine annual salaries of all staff members and the Advisory Council shall determine Annual salaries for Pastors, these shall be sanctioned yearly or more frequently if necessary. These salaries should be paid weekly unless agreed upon otherwise by the Pastor of the local Church. Love offerings may be given at the benevolence of members of the congregation or community but must by accurately accounted for in the financial ledger of each local assembly. In addition, there shall also be fund raising gathered for collective projects for the Church and its growth and mission and community outreach will be included. A percentage of the each assembly's collections will be decided upon by each local church to sow into National Ministries and World Missions.

B. Non-Pastoral Church workers such as clerks, typists, messengers etc. shall be considered self employed will be personally responsible to pay tax according to the laws of the land and shall be hired as consultant positions in the local church until the church is able to handle full time employees and staff which shall be determined by the Local Presbytery.

C. This church has the authority to establish foundations for the welfare of humans in such capacities as health, education, shelter and other humanitarian needs. Each shall have the power to receive endowments donations, monetary and non-monetary items such as materials or land. All investments and receiving of none monetary items must be approved by the Presbytery and all investments will be determined by an outside investment firm to assure that no personal agenda is being entertained by any member of the organization. No contributor may dictate the use of any funds or lands, materials or endowments without a written agreement from the Local Presbytery upon it's acceptance of the gift. All contributions will be freely distributed to the present needs of the Church as the Pastor and Local Presbytery deem necessary.

D. The finances of the ministry shall be obtained through tithes, offerings and donations and endowments

E. The Local Presbytery shall have power to raise loans from the bank or other secured financial institutions for the development of the church, evangelism or mission and outreach projects as the need for such development arises.

F. The church shall have the right to all property, real or chattel, shall be take, hold sell, transfer, lease, rent, mortgage, or convey in the name of_____ Church . It shall be solely responsible for its own financial liabilities. Such ventures into contracts and financial agreements shall be approved by the Local Presbytery and should be sent for review before engaging in them to the Advisory Council to provide stability and accountability and for added accuracy and caution. Final decisions to enter contracts and agreement will rest solely in the power of the Local Presbytery following the Advisory Council's recommendations.

CHAPTER TEN

FELLOWSHIPS AND OVERSIGHT

This section of your By Laws will be determined based upon whether or not your ministry will have more than one location and whether or not you will start other works that you will want to have oversight of them. At first you may want to have a stronger cohesiveness in the beginning and then bring it to a more limited oversight but remember that accountability is a must for a healthy and cooperative ministry. If you would like a sample of a set of By Laws that have a government structure under one Overseer, those By Laws may also be requested for further review if you write to this ministry.

The articles listed in these particular By Laws will give a guideline a founder's dream to continue once delegated authority begins. As we know there must be one vision for every ministry and without that vision being made clear the people will perish. If everyone has their own vision then many problems will arise but if one vision is fulfilled and other men run with that one and selfsame vision there is nothing that shall be impossible. Since you are adding a second governing council for only some key and specific things to insure stability and integrity, you must define very clearly how much or how little they will be involved. As you will see in the following Article 23 only limited authority is given to this Council of ministers. However, In the beginning stages of a ministry you can give them more control if you so choose and can replace them in the By Laws where the Local Presbytery is stated. These were developed with limited authority after 4 to 5 years of service of ministers under the founder being sure that the ministers with them were sound and men and women of integrity.

Only you as a leader know who is among you and who is capable to lead. Be sure that these individuals are not only able and willing to lead but have a heart of servant-hood to one vision and not their own agenda. In our situation we thought it necessary after giving full power to the local church in almost all areas of government structure that there were some things that still needed other outside eyes and ears to continue to have a voice for the well being of the local Pastor, the founder, and the congregations that have been raised up.

One very important issue is that of determining the annual salary of a Pastor. I discussed this issue in the beginning of this book. Financial reviews are also important for stability. Doctrinal soundness is the third issue and who may hold credentials is the last.

Listed below you will find these requirements spelled out for your consideration.

ARTICLE 23:

REQUIREMENTS FOR MINISTERS AND CHURCHES IN THIS FELLOWSHIP:

This Local church body shall be self-governing by the articles listed in this document. The Advisory Council of ministers shall reside over these churches to keep honest men honest and give spiritual guidance to those who carry the vision of the Founder

_____.

This council will be appointed by (founder's name)_____ and shall be in the number of ___ to ___ members of licensed and ordained ministers. (Generally 5 to 7 members)

This Advisory Council shall be empowered to:

- Determine annual salaries and reimbursement policies for the ministers.
- Review financial reporting quarterly submitted by the local church treasurers and offer council and recommendations for better stewardship of the finances recorded if necessary to the Local Presbytery.
- This Council will be available to safe guard a congregation in the case of a minister gone array ethically or in his or her integrity or in the case where a pastor does not fulfill his or her calling or becomes doctrinally unsound. This council has the ability to

intervene to bring order and correction to the minister and aid to the local church.

- These members of the Advisory Council may call a meeting to discuss any issues with the pastors that they deem necessary at any time. This is to ensure sound doctrine and ethical practices within the local churches that exhibits' utmost integrity and holiness among leaders.
- This council may retract ministerial credentials if the pastor of the local church does not exhibit a divine calling or character above reproach as set forth in the qualifications of pastor in these documents.
- This council must approve licenses of any minister applying for license from any of the local churches of this fellowship as well as any other ministers who will be sent out from these churches with license or ordination.

CHAPTER ELEVEN

DISCIPLINE OF LEADERS

In this final chapter I want to address a very important issue. Due to the nature of our present ministerial problems in today's society, I believe that Article 24 is not one that can be ignored from its placement in the By Laws. There has been such a break down in the areas of church and ministerial ethics that it is frightening to think of the Day of Judgment. Many Independent Ministers have put their own selves in vulnerable positions and have become the enemies feeding ground. I say that these things must be obverted. We have a responsibility that is so great in the eyes of men and of God. It must be safe guarded.

When it comes to dealing with leaders found in rebellion or sin or any other type of misrepresentation they must be handled both delicately and purposefully guarding the lives of precious and innocent people. There are many founders of ministries that go off both morally and doctrinally but because they are the "leader" no one can correct them and many lives are destroyed. If someone has the right heart in the beginning of things it would be his or her duty to safe guard even themselves from being prey to the enemy.

Dealing with Discipline is a very important issue and should not be taken lightly. One must always have the best interest of all persons in mind. If these guidelines are not stated then you cannot enforce them when necessary without a court battle which only damages more people. You may also be accused of slander or lose your own reputation in the midst of trying to correct a problem. These guidelines will help you to act upon proper Biblical Discipline when necessary in your organization. Even though you may be independent, you as a leader should still have someone who is able to "step in" on behalf of your sheep if you should ever go off. That is just love!

Then we must continue in this article to give a step by step as to how a vacancy should there be one will be filled. This is very important as well. You may write out even clearer guidelines and policies in detail for different scenarios as a separate document if you deem it necessary. This can only be determined by the nature of the environment you are in as well as the types of outreach you may venture into.

ARTICLE 24:

DISCIPLINARY ACTION FOR PASTORAL AND LEADERSHIP OFFICES:

Section 1.

Any Pastor may be removed or suspended from his/her position as well as the Presbytery or Advisory Council he/she may hold by a committee appointed by the Advisory Council and such action affirmed by the majority vote of the remaining Elders or ministers of _____. The reason for such action will be as follows; If this committee concludes that s/he is not conducting her/himself in the best interests of this Church or that her/his behavior or attitude may be characterized by any of the following Scriptural classification: a) Those who reject a part or whole of the doctrine of Christ (2 John 9-11) b.) Those guilty of immorality (1Cor. 5:9-11); c) Those who are unruly or walk disorderly (2 Th 3:6-12); d) Those who cause division (Rom 16:16); e. Those who are domineering, quarrelsome or sectarian (3John 9-10); or f) Those who defile who defile their separation from the world (Jas 4:4; Rev. 2:20-22).

Sub-Section 1:

Any Pastor may be suspended from office by the Advisory council and a majority affirming vote of that council at any council meeting called for such purpose or as provided in Article 23- C. For any of the following causes which are hereby declared to be contrary and damaging to the best interests of this Church organization:

1. Gross or willful neglect of the duties of her/his office.

2. Failure or refusal to disclose necessary information on matters of the business affairs or ministries of any other services or enterprises or activities of this Church.

3. Unauthorized expenditures, abuse or unauthorized use of credit, unauthorized signing of checks, or other misuse of funds of this church.

4. Unwarranted attacks on any of the other members of this church council, or refusal to cooperate with the other officers and or their ministries or services or other enterprises of this church.

5. Misrepresentation of this church and or of any of its Elders to outside persons or churches or associations or societies.

6. Mental illness or incapacity, or dishonesty, or immoral or fraudulent or unchristian or heretic conduct.

7. Conviction of a felony.

8. Membership in or cooperation or identity with any subversive organization or society or group or association.

9. Participation of any kind of disseminating propaganda or otherwise attempting to influence or to intervene in any political campaign on behalf of any candidate for public office or any public issue, in the name of or involving the influence of the church.

Section 2:

Filling of Vacancies.

During such investigation, a Pastor will be removed from all forms of leadership immediately. Upon the removal or suspension of a Pastor a resident Elder or interim Pastor may be appointed by the Advisory council until the matter is resolved. Except as otherwise provided in these bylaws, any vacancy occurring in any office by reason of death, resignation, disqualification, exclusion or otherwise, may be filled, protem, by any member of the advisory council or appointment of the advisory council and affirmed by a three fourths vote of that council and inclusion of all other ministers of LWCC organization.

<u>Sub- Section 2:</u>

Upon the removal or suspension of any Pastor from his post and any other office which he/she may hold, he/she shall be notified by the council in writing of the action taken, and her/his exclusion or suspension shall be effective as of the date of such notice, and such action shall be final and non-appeal-able until the investigation and ruling is completed by the Advisory Council.

It is essential that an authority represent God rigidly. Whenever we execute God's authority and take care of His kingdom, we have to do it with fear and trembling and above reproach. It is my belief that man should not do anything out of what he personally thinks is right or wrong. Rather, he should do all things out of obedience to the Word of God as the standard. All authority is appointed by God and everything is ordered by Him. If we truly trace any authority upward, we will never end with a man but we will eventually come to God. God is the highest authority and all men must be subject to Him. If we are subject to Him, we will also be subject to one another no matter what our position is. Whether our position is high or low it is ordered by God and we must submit ourselves one to another in the fear of God who is our greatest authority. God is a God of order and a God of submission. All men must have a heart of submission who serves Him. Let us humble ourselves before our Sovereign God and let us all remain teachable as is the character of a Godly leader.

As we bring this book to an end remember, God has commissioned you to fulfill the great commission. He has called you and set you apart for a work not made with human hands. You are to be clay in His hands to fulfill His divine will. None of us who are in ministry came into it by choice. We were chosen. Having been chosen, let us do all that we can with integrity and honor to further the kingdom of heaven.

Set your house in order and your ministry and it will be well with you my fellow servant in the fields of souls. Go with God and go with the Gospel and go with understanding to achieve more than you ever dreamed possible! By HIS GRACE ALONE!

It is my prayer that this will assist you as you walk out God's divine purpose and will for your life.

Made in the USA
Middletown, DE
19 April 2021